It Only Starts with One Word

YOUR WORDS HURT ME

Malachi Overcomes His Past for a Better Future

by ALLEN BROWN

BUILD OUR KINGDOM PUBLISHING
—— BUILD OUR KINGDOM.COM ——

Your Words Hurt Me

Printed in the United States of America

1st Edition January 2025 First Printing

ISBN for paperback: 978-1-964203-17-1

Build Our Kingdom Publishing, LLC. 560 Main St, Stroudsburg, PA 18360

Edited by: Allen Brown

Although the publisher and the author have made every effort to ensure that the information in this book was correct at press time and while this publication is designed to provide accurate information in regard to the subject matter covered, the publisher and the author assume no responsibility for errors, inaccuracies, omissions, or any other inconsistencies herein and hereby disclaim any liability to any party for any loss, damage, or disruption caused by errors or omissions, whether such errors or omissions result from negligence, accident, or any other cause.

This publication is meant as a source of valuable information for the reader, however, it is not meant as a substitute for direct expert assistance. If such a level of assistance is required, the services of a competent professional should be sought.

Table of Contents

iv

Dedication

This book is dedicated to everyone who has ever carried the weight of words—both the ones spoken to you and the ones you've whispered to yourself.

To those who have overcome the words that tried to break them, may you continue to walk in confidence, knowing that your story is greater than the lies once told about you.

And to those still struggling with the echoes of the past, know this: words may hurt, but they do not have to define you.

It is our prayer that the message within these pages brings healing, hope, and the strength to believe in yourself again. You are more than what has been said about you. You are worthy, capable, and powerful.

Choose your words wisely. And most of all—choose the right ones to believe.

~ Allen Brown ~

Acknowledgment

I want to sincerely thank everyone who contributed to this book—whether through encouragement, feedback, or simply believing in the message behind it.

To my family, friends, and supporters, your words and support have meant everything.

To the readers, thank you for taking this journey with Malachi. May this book remind you that **your story is still being written, and the words you choose today can shape a better tomorrow.**

Introduction:

The Words That Shaped Me

I never really thought much about words. Not really.

People say things all the time. Some words feel good—like when my teachcr told me I was smart, or when my best friend said I was funny. But other words stick in a different way. Words that don't feel so good.

Like when my mom used to say, *"You're going to be just like your father."*

I didn't even know my father. I still don't. But the way she said it—it wasn't like a compliment. It was like a warning. Like I was already messing up.

Or when she'd tell me, *"You'll never be more than a regular worker."*

At the time, I didn't know what that meant. I was just a kid. But now, looking back, I realize those words got stuck inside me. They made me afraid to dream too big.

And then there's the saying everyone knows: *"Sticks and stones may break my bones, but words will never hurt me."*

That's a lie. I know because I've been hit with a rock before. I was playing outside with my friend Billy, and he accidentally threw one too hard. It hurt—a lot—but after a little while, the pain went away.

I've also fallen off the swings and scraped my arm on the ground. That left a scar, but I don't even think about it anymore.

But the words?

The words stayed.

Even now, when I try something new, I hear my mom's voice in my head: *"You'll never be more than this."*

Even now, when I want to do something exciting, I remember her warning: *"You could get hurt."*

Even now, when someone gives me a compliment, I wonder if they really mean it.

Words don't just disappear. They stick to you, shape you, change how you see yourself.

So, I want to tell you my story.

2

I want to show you how words shaped my world. How the things people said to me—at home, at school, with my friends, and later in life—built the way I saw myself.

And maybe, as you read, you'll think about the words in your world too.

Because words can hurt. But maybe—just maybe—if we understand them, we can change the way thcy shape us.

Chapter 1

First Words

I don't remember much from when I was a baby. I mean, who does? But I've been told things. And some of those things—some of those words—stuck with me.

For as early as I can remember, my mom used to say, *"Boy, don't make me hurt you."* I wasn't trying to do anything wrong. Most of the time, I was just playing, having fun like any kid would. But those words made me feel nervous, like I always had to be careful.

Whenever I got in trouble, she would say, *"Stop crying before I give you something to cry about."* But I was already crying. I was already hurting. So what did she mean? Did she think I wasn't hurt enough?

And then there was the one that I heard all the time: *"You're so bad."*

I didn't feel bad. I wasn't trying to be bad. I was just being a kid. But when you hear something enough times, you start to wonder if it's true.

I do remember sometimes my mom would say, *"Good boy."* But it was only when I did exactly what she wanted. It wasn't the kind of praise that made me feel proud—it just felt like the only way to avoid getting in trouble. It didn't make me feel free to just be myself.

I remember visiting my Aunt Susan's house once. I was curious about something on the table, so I reached for it. Before I could even understand what was happening, she popped my hand and snapped, *"Don't do that!"* It scared me. I didn't even know I had done something wrong. But that moment stuck with me.

After that, I became more careful about touching things. More cautious. Less curious.

I don't remember when I said my first word, but I've always been told that it was *"No."* And apparently, I got in trouble for saying it a lot. But how does a two-year-old get in trouble for saying *no* when that's one of the only words they know? I was just learning, wasn't I?

As I got older and learned to talk more, I started noticing something else.

People didn't always like when I spoke.

My siblings would tell me, *"You talk too much."* Or they'd laugh and say, *"You sound so silly."* I thought it was okay to express myself. I thought it was okay to share how I felt. But I started to realize that maybe it wasn't. Maybe it was better to stay quiet.

I had happy times growing up. A lot of them. But when I think about some of the words that were said to me, I can't help but feel sad.

Because words didn't just come and go like the wind. They stayed.

I didn't realize it then, but those words were shaping me. Some words told me I was liked, maybe even loved. Some words were warnings—reminders to be careful. And some words made me feel like I wasn't good enough.

Even before I understood everything, I was learning what words meant. I could tell, just by how someone said something—or how many times they said it—whether it was good or bad.

And I was learning what those words meant about me.

Chapter 2

Meeting Rebecca – A New Perspective

I didn't think much about words before I met Rebecca.

At home, words were warnings, reminders of what I did wrong, or just things people said when they were frustrated. They weren't things that made you feel good—not really. They were just part of life.

But then, in sixth grade, I met **her**.

She was different from anyone I had ever met before. Her name was Rebecca, and she was one of those people who always seemed happy. The kind of happy that made you wonder if she knew something the rest of us didn't.

The first time she spoke to me, I thought she was joking.

"Hey, Malachi, I like your handwriting. It's really neat."

I blinked at her, unsure if she was talking to me or the person next to me. Nobody ever told me stuff like that. I shrugged.

"Uh... thanks?"

She smiled like I had said something funny.

"No, really. It looks cool. Mine is a mess." She held up her notebook, where her letters stretched across the page in big, loopy strokes.

I didn't know what to say. Usually, when people talked to me, it was to tell me I was doing something wrong. But Rebecca? She just... said nice things. Like it was normal.

At first, I didn't know what to do with that.

A Different Kind of Person

Rebecca wasn't like the kids I usually hung around. She was always talking, always smiling. It wasn't the loud, in-your-face kind of happy. It was just... light. Like she didn't carry the weight of words the way I did.

She laughed easily. She asked a million questions. She had this way of saying *"You got this!"* that actually made you believe it.

And she noticed things.

"You're really good at math, Malachi."

"You always remember stuff—how do you do that?"

"I like how you explain things; you make them easy to understand."

At first, I thought she was just being nice. But she wasn't saying these things like she *had* to—she said them like she actually meant them. Like she saw something in me I didn't even see in myself.

Home vs. School

At school, Rebecca's words were like a fresh breeze. But at home? It was the same as always.

"Why are you always so quiet?"

"You're just like your father."

"You think you're smart, but you don't know anything."

No matter how many times I heard Rebecca's voice at school, the voices at home were louder.

It felt like I was living two different lives. At school, around Rebecca, I almost felt normal—like maybe I wasn't as bad as I had always thought. But at home, those same old words pulled me back down.

A Small Shift

One day, we were sitting outside at recess when Rebecca turned to me and said, *"You know, I think you'd be good at writing stories."*

I laughed. *"Nah, I'm not really good at stuff like that."*

She frowned. *"Says who?"*

The question caught me off guard. *Says who?* I had never thought about that before.

I started to tell her that nobody in my family ever did anything like that, that I wasn't the kind of person who could be "good" at something. But then I stopped. Because the truth was... the only people who had ever said that were the ones who had never really seen me.

Rebecca saw me differently.

And even though I wasn't ready to believe her yet, for the first time, I *wondered* if she could be right.

End of Chapter Reflection

Malachi is introduced to a different way of speaking—one that lifts people up instead of tearing them down.

He still doesn't fully believe Rebecca's words, but they challenge the way he's always thought about himself.

He starts to see the contrast between home and school, between the words that pull him down and the ones that try to lift him up.

A small seed of doubt is planted—maybe everything he's believed about himself *isn't* the full truth.

Chapter 3

The Words That Break You

Sixth grade was supposed to be better.

I had met Rebecca. She was nice to me—nicer than most people ever were. She talked to me like I mattered, like she actually saw something good in me. It was weird, but in a way that made me feel… okay.

But then, Jeff showed up.

Jeff was the kind of kid that everyone either wanted to be or wanted to be friends with. He was loud, confident, and never seemed to care what anyone thought of him. He joked around all the time, but the problem was, his jokes weren't always funny—especially when they were about me.

The first time it happened, we were all standing in line after lunch, waiting to go back to class. Rebecca was next to me, talking about some book she was reading, when Jeff walked up and smirked.

"You don't want to be talking to him," he said to her, loud enough for everyone nearby to hear. *"You want me. Look at him—he's ugly."*

A few kids around us laughed.

I felt my stomach drop. I knew I wasn't the best-looking kid in school, but hearing someone say it out loud—especially in front of Rebecca—made my face burn.

Rebecca rolled her eyes. *"Oh, stop, Jeff."* She said it like she wasn't taking him seriously, but I couldn't ignore the way everyone else was still smiling, waiting to see what Jeff would say next.

"Nah, for real," he continued. *"Why you hanging around him? He's all quiet and weird. You need a real dude, not some little nerd."*

More laughs.

I swallowed, trying to act like it didn't bother me. Like it was just words. But something about the way everyone was looking at me made me want to disappear.

I didn't say anything. What was I supposed to say? If I clapped back, Jeff would just throw another joke at me. If I walked away,

16

I'd look weak. And if I pretended it didn't matter, no one would believe me—because it did.

It really did.

The Echo of Words

That wasn't the only time Jeff went at me.

Sometimes, it was little things—like how he'd nudge me in the hallway and say, *"Move, loser."* Or when he'd see me sitting with Rebecca and make jokes about how I'd never get a girl like her.

Other times, it was worse.

"Yo, you ever think about getting a haircut? Maybe then you wouldn't look so lame."

"I bet you cry at night, huh? Look at him, he probably cries himself to sleep."

"Man, you ain't gonna be nothing when you grow up. You might as well quit now."

He always said it like he was joking. But the thing about jokes is that sometimes they weren't really jokes at all.

And the worst part?

Some of the things Jeff said weren't that different from what I had already heard at home.

"You won't be nothing."

"You're not good enough."

"You're weak."

But at home, it was just family. I could hide it.

At school?

Everyone heard it.

And for the first time, I wasn't just thinking those things in my head—I was *feeling* them. Every time Jeff spoke, it was like a little crack in my confidence.

And after a while, I stopped fighting it.

Maybe he was right.

Maybe I wasn't much of anything.

Rebecca's Reminder

One day, after another one of Jeff's comments, I sat alone at recess, pretending to look busy so no one would bother me.

Rebecca sat down next to me.

"You okay?" she asked.

I shrugged. *"Yeah. Just tired."*

She tilted her head, watching me.

"You know he's wrong, right?"

I scoffed. *"Who?"*

"Jeff."

I didn't answer. Because honestly, I wasn't sure if she was right.

"I don't know why you listen to him," she said. *"He just likes to run his mouth. That doesn't mean he knows anything about you."*

I kept staring at the ground. *"Yeah, well... maybe he's not wrong."*

Rebecca sighed.

"Malachi, don't do that. Don't believe stuff just because someone says it loud enough."

I wanted to believe her. I really did. But it wasn't that easy.

"It's different for you," I muttered. *"Nobody says that stuff to you."*

She nudged my arm. *"That's not true. People say things to me, too."*

I finally looked at her. *"Yeah, but it doesn't bother you."*

She gave me a small smile. *"It used to."*

I frowned. I had never thought about that before.

"But one day, I decided something," she continued. *"Just because someone says something about you doesn't make it true. Words only have power if you let them."*

I nodded like I understood, but deep down, I wasn't sure I believed that yet.

Because no matter what she said, Jeff's words still felt true.

End of Chapter Reflection

- **Jeff is introduced as the first direct challenge to Malachi's self-esteem.** His words reinforce the things Malachi has already struggled with, but now in a public way.

- **Malachi starts to withdraw.** For the first time, the words aren't just things he hears—they're things he starts to believe.

- **Rebecca provides a counterbalance.** She tries to encourage him, but Malachi isn't ready to fully believe her yet.

- **The idea of choice is introduced.** Rebecca plants the idea that words only have power if you let them—but Malachi isn't there yet.

Chapter 4

The Fear of Failing

I wanted to quit before I even started.

Trying out for the basketball team seemed like a good idea at first. I wasn't the best, but I could hold my own. And for once, I thought maybe I'd have something to be proud of. Something that could prove I wasn't just the quiet kid, the kid people overlooked, or the one Jeff always made fun of.

But as soon as I walked into the gym, I knew I didn't belong.

The other guys were already there, dribbling, shooting, laughing. They all knew each other. They had been playing together for years. I was just some kid trying to take up space on their team.

I picked up a ball and started dribbling near the sideline, trying not to draw attention to myself. But it didn't matter.

"Yo, who's that?" one of the players asked.

"That's Malachi," Jeff said, smirking. Of course, he was here. *"Don't worry, he won't be here long."*

I clenched my jaw but didn't say anything.

The Pressure of the Game

The coach blew his whistle, and tryouts officially started. We were split into teams for drills—passing, shooting, running plays. I knew the moves. I had practiced enough in my driveway to know I could handle it.

But the words were already in my head.

"You don't want him."

"He's not good enough."

"Look at him, he's weak."

Every time I went for a pass, I hesitated. Every time I had a shot, I second-guessed it. Every time I made a mistake, I felt the eyes on me, waiting to laugh.

And then it happened.

I got the ball at the top of the key. I had a wide-open shot. For a split second, I thought about taking it. I should have taken it.

But I didn't.

Instead, I passed it off—too fast, too careless. The ball slipped through my teammate's hands and bounced out of bounds.

24

"Come on, man!" one of the guys groaned.

"What was that?" another muttered.

Jeff chuckled. *"Told y'all."*

My face burned.

I had the shot. And I didn't take it.

Not because I couldn't.

But because I had already convinced myself I was going to miss.

Not Giving It My All

For the rest of tryouts, I played like a shadow of myself. I did just enough to not embarrass myself completely. I ran the plays, I made the passes, but I never took a real shot. I never went all in.

Because in my head, I had already lost.

When it was over, the coach read off the names of the players who made the team. I held my breath.

And then…

"Malachi."

I made it.

I should have been excited. But instead, all I felt was relief. Not because I wanted to be here.

But because I didn't want to be the kid who quit.

I didn't want to look weak.

But deep down, I knew the truth.

I *was* weak. Not because I wasn't good enough. Not because I didn't have the skills.

But because I let words beat me before I ever stepped on the court.

End of Chapter Reflection

- **Malachi struggles with self-doubt before he even tries.** He lets the words of others shape his confidence before he has a chance to prove himself.

- **He plays safe, afraid to make mistakes.** Instead of playing with heart, he does just enough to get by—never fully committing because he's already convinced himself he'll fail.

- **He doesn't quit, but he doesn't win either.** He makes the team, but it doesn't feel like a victory. He realizes that words don't just hurt—they *limit* him.

- **The setup for Rebecca's return.** Malachi is stuck in his own head, believing the worst about himself. But soon, Rebecca will step in and remind him of what he's capable of.

Chapter 5

The Words That Lift You Up

I wasn't in the mood to talk about basketball.

Tryouts had been over for a few days, and all I could think about was what I *could have* done. The shot I should have taken. The plays I should have made. I had made the team, but it didn't feel like a win.

So when Rebecca waved me down after school and said, *"Hey! So? Did you make it?"* I almost didn't want to answer.

I shrugged. *"Yeah."*

Her face lit up. *"That's awesome! I knew you'd make it!"*

I let out a small laugh. *"Yeah, well…"*

"What?" she asked, tilting her head.

"I could've done better," I admitted.

Rebecca frowned. *"What do you mean? You made the team!"*

"Yeah, but I didn't play like I should have. I second-guessed everything. Every time I got the ball, I thought about all the stuff

people were saying about me. And instead of proving them wrong, I kinda... just played it safe."

Rebecca nodded like she understood. *"Okay. So you didn't give it your best. But you know what that means?"*

"That I messed up?"

"No," she said. *"That you can do better. You're already on the team. Now, all that stuff in your head? You don't need to listen to it anymore."*

I sighed. *"Yeah, well, that's easier for you. Nobody talks about you the way people talk about me."*

Rebecca folded her arms. *"That's not true."*

I raised an eyebrow. *"Really?"*

She gave a small smile. *"Yep. You know what people used to say to me? They called me annoying. They told me I talk too much. That I was 'too much' for some people. And for a while, I let that get to me. I started being quieter, not speaking up, trying to be 'less' so people wouldn't say anything."*

"But you're not like that now," I pointed out.

She nodded. *"Because one day, I realized something. Those words weren't mine to keep. They were just things people said. I get to decide what words I believe about myself."*

I sat with that for a second. *"So, what? I'm just supposed to ignore everything people say?"*

"No," she said. *"You're supposed to decide which words matter."*

I thought back to Jeff, to the guys on the team, to all the things I had let sink into me.

Then I thought about Rebecca, about how she never talked to me the way they did.

Maybe she was right. Maybe I had been giving too much power to the wrong words.

"Well, either way, I still don't know if I should've made the team," I muttered.

Rebecca grinned. *"Too late, you're on it! So now, you don't have to think about whether you belong—you just have to show up and prove it to yourself."*

For the first time since tryouts, I smiled.

Maybe I wasn't sure about myself yet.

But Rebecca was.

And maybe—just maybe—that was enough to start.

End of Chapter Reflection

- **Rebecca brings encouragement back into Malachi's life.** She reminds him that just because negative words are said doesn't mean they have to be true.

- **Malachi realizes he has been holding onto the wrong words.** He starts questioning what he believes about himself.

- **The idea of choice grows stronger.** Rebecca plants the idea that he gets to decide which words he lets define him.

- **This chapter transitions Malachi into the next phase.** He's still struggling, but he's starting to challenge his negative thoughts. Soon, those thoughts will be tested even more—especially when he enters the world of dating.

Chapter 6

The Words You Can't Believe

By the time I hit eighth grade, things were different.

I had grown a little. Gotten taller. My voice was deeper. I wasn't the same quiet little kid from sixth grade.

But in my head?

I still was.

No matter how much I changed on the outside, I still heard the same words in my head. *"You don't want him, you want me." "He's ugly." "He's weird."* Jeff's voice never really left me. And because of that, I never really thought of myself as someone a girl would actually like.

So when Rebecca overheard something at lunch, I wasn't ready for it.

The Unexpected Compliment

I was sitting at our usual table, picking at my tray, when Rebecca plopped down next to me with a smirk.

"Guess what I just heard?"

I glanced at her. *"What?"*

"Jayla thinks you're cute."

I froze.

"What?"

"Yup," she said, grinning. *"I just heard her tell Brianna. She actually said it! 'Malachi is cute.'"*

I shook my head, laughing under my breath. *"Yeah, okay."*

Rebecca frowned. *"I'm serious. Why don't you believe me?"*

"Because that's not true."

"Says who?"

"Says reality."

Rebecca rolled her eyes. *"You know what? I think you need proof."*

Before I could stop her, she stood up and waved Jayla over.

My stomach dropped.

The Moment He Can't Accept

Jayla walked over, looking a little nervous. *"Hey, Rebecca said you wanted to talk to me?"*

Rebecca elbowed me.

I swallowed hard. *"Uh, no, I mean—"*

"It's okay," Jayla said with a small smile. *"I just… I just wanted to say I think you're really cute."*

Silence.

I stared at her, waiting for the joke. Waiting for Jeff to pop out of nowhere and start laughing. Waiting for the moment where she would take it back and say, *"Nah, I was just kidding."*

But she didn't.

She just stood there, waiting for me to say something back.

But I couldn't.

Because everything in me was screaming that this wasn't real. That she must be messing with me. That no one would actually mean that.

So instead of saying thank you, instead of smiling, instead of believing her…

I shrugged. *"Okay."*

Her smile faded. *"Oh. Well... okay then."*

She walked away, and Rebecca groaned.

"Are you serious?!" she whisper-yelled. *"Malachi! She actually likes you!"*

I shook my head. *"Nah, she was just being nice."*

"No, she wasn't! Why do you do that?"

I looked down at my tray.

"Because I already know the truth."

The Words That Stuck

The truth was, I *wanted* to believe Jayla.

I wanted to believe I was worth liking.

But I couldn't. Because the words that had been spoken to me before had already settled in my head.

And those words—the ones from Jeff, the ones from home, the ones I had replayed over and over—were louder than Jayla's.

It wasn't that I didn't want to date her.

It was that I didn't believe it would last.

Because how could I keep someone who actually liked me, if I never believed I was worth liking in the first place?

Rebecca's Encouragement

After lunch, Rebecca caught up with me.

"Malachi, you have to stop doing this to yourself."

"Doing what?"

"Pushing people away because you won't believe anything good about yourself."

I sighed. *"It's not that easy, Becca."*

She softened. *"I know. But just because people said stuff about you doesn't mean it's true. You believe Jeff over me. Over Jayla. Why?"*

I didn't have an answer.

"Words don't have to define you, Malachi," she said gently. *"But you're the one who decides which ones do."*

End of Chapter Reflection

- **Malachi struggles to accept compliments.** Even when someone likes him, he pushes it away because he doesn't believe it.

- **The words from his past are stronger than the words in his present.** He lets negative voices overpower the positive ones.

- **Rebecca tries to help him see the truth.** But Malachi isn't ready to believe it just yet.

- **This sets up the next phase of his journey.** He's growing, but his insecurities still hold him back.

Chapter 7

The Words That Ruin Things

I never thought I'd actually get a girlfriend.

Even after Jayla, even after Rebecca kept telling me to believe in myself, I still carried those doubts with me. But somehow, I ended up in a relationship. Somehow, I got close to someone who actually liked me, and for a little while… it felt good.

Her name was **Alyssa**.

She wasn't loud or flashy. She wasn't one of those girls who needed attention all the time. She was just… easy to talk to. She laughed at my jokes. She asked me questions like she actually cared what I had to say. And most of all, she liked being around me.

Me.

At first, I didn't let myself think too hard about it. I just enjoyed it. We texted all the time. We sat together at lunch. Sometimes we walked home from school together, just talking. For once, I felt normal.

But the thing about words—the bad ones, the ones that got stuck in my head—is that they never really go away.

And even when everything was good, those words still found a way to creep back in.

The Doubts That Never Left

A few months into our relationship, I started to notice little things.

If she took a little longer to text back, I wondered if she was losing interest. If she laughed a little too hard at someone else's joke, I felt like I wasn't good enough. If she didn't say something nice about me that day, I wondered if she was realizing I wasn't as great as she thought I was.

Because deep down, I was waiting for her to leave.

Not because she said she would.

But because I thought she eventually *would*.

Self-Sabotage

One day, we were sitting together at lunch, and I wasn't really talking.

"What's up with you today?" Alyssa asked, nudging me.

I shrugged. *"Nothing."*

"Come on, Malachi. You've been weird all week."

I sighed, debating whether to say what was really on my mind.

"I just... I don't know why you're even with me."

She blinked. *"What?"*

"I mean, you could be with anybody. Someone funnier, or better looking, or whatever. You're probably gonna leave me anyway."

Her face twisted like I had just insulted her.

"Why would you say that?"

I shrugged again. *"It's just the truth."*

Alyssa crossed her arms. *"No, it's not. You just think it is. And honestly, it's kinda messed up that you don't believe me when I say I like you."*

I swallowed hard. *"I'm just being real."*

"No, you're not," she snapped. *"You're making me feel like I have to prove something to you every single day just because you don't believe in yourself."*

I didn't know what to say.

"I can tell you how much I like you, I can show you, but if you don't believe it, then what am I even doing here?"

I stared at my tray.

"You're not gonna mess this up, are you?" she asked, her voice softer now.

I wanted to say no. I wanted to fix it. But I didn't know *how.*

Because in my head, I had already lost her.

And a week later, I did.

The Breakup

It wasn't one big fight. It wasn't anything dramatic.

One day, Alyssa just stopped trying.

Stopped texting first.

Stopped sitting next to me.

Stopped asking me what was wrong.

And I couldn't even blame her.

Because every time she tried to love me, I pushed her away.

Every time she gave me good words, I drowned them out with the bad ones that were already inside me.

And eventually, she got tired of fighting a battle that I was losing on my own.

Rebecca's I-Told-You-So Moment

"So, she dumped you."

I shot Rebecca a look. *"Gee, thanks."*

She smirked. *"I'm not saying 'I told you so'..."*

"But you're totally saying 'I told you so.'"

She sighed. *"Malachi, I'm serious. How many times do I have to tell you that you can't let those old words control you?"*

I didn't answer.

"Look, I get it," she said, softer now. *"You've been told a lot of messed-up things. But at some point, you have to decide if you're gonna keep believing them... or if you're gonna believe the people who actually care about you."*

I ran a hand over my face. *"I don't know how."*

43

"You start by listening."

"Listening to what?"

"To the right words."

End of Chapter Reflection

- **Malachi's past words ruin his relationship.** Even though Alyssa genuinely likes him, he can't accept it.
- **Self-sabotage plays a role.** Instead of believing in the good, he convinces himself things will fail—so they do.
- **Rebecca steps in to remind him of his choices.** She tries to help him understand that *he* is the one keeping himself from happiness.
- **This sets up the next phase of Malachi's journey.** Now that he's lost something real, will he finally learn to fight back against the words that control him?

Chapter 8

The Words That Hold You Back

Getting a job was supposed to be simple.

I wasn't trying to do anything crazy. I just wanted to make some money after school, maybe save up for some things of my own. But when it actually came time to fill out applications, to walk into stores and ask if they were hiring, something in me froze.

I kept staring at the blank spaces on the form—"Skills," "Work Experience," "Why do you want to work here?"—and my mind kept repeating the same words.

"Your father was a failure."

"He couldn't keep a job."

"You're just like him."

I had never even met my father. I didn't know what kind of man he really was. But my mom's words made sure I believed I already knew everything I needed to.

And if I was just like him, then what was the point of trying?

Introducing Phillip—The Mentor

I was sitting outside the corner store, staring at a *Now Hiring* sign in the window, when Phillip walked up.

"What's up, Malachi?" he said, nodding as he took a sip from his drink.

Phillip wasn't a teacher or a coach. He wasn't one of my classmates, either. He was just a guy from the neighborhood—a couple years older, already working, already making moves. He had a job at the auto shop down the street, and people liked him. He always had something going on, always seemed to have a plan.

"Not much," I muttered.

He followed my gaze to the sign.

"You thinking about applying?"

I hesitated. *"I dunno."*

"Why not? It's just a job."

I sighed. *"What if I mess it up?"*

Phillip frowned. *"Mess it up how? It's not that deep."*

I shrugged, feeling stupid for even saying it out loud. But something about Phillip made me want to keep talking.

"My mom used to say my dad couldn't keep a job. That he was a failure. And I guess... I don't know. What if I'm the same way?"

Phillip let out a low whistle. *"Man, who told you that? Your mom?"*

I nodded.

He took another sip of his drink, then shook his head. *"Alright, let me ask you something. Did you ever see your dad lose a job?"*

I blinked. *"What?"*

"Did you ever watch your dad go to work and get fired? Did you ever see him quit?"

"No... I mean, I never met him."

"Exactly." Phillip leaned back. *"So how do you know it's true?"*

I stared at him.

"Look, man," he continued. *"People say a lot of things. Sometimes because they believe it. Sometimes because they're mad. And sometimes because they don't know how to say what*

they really feel. But that don't mean you gotta take it as your truth."

I swallowed.

"You ever change a tire?" he asked suddenly.

I frowned. *"What? No."*

"You ever tried?"

"No."

"Okay, so what if I told you you suck at changing tires?"

I let out a small laugh. *"I guess you could be right."*

"Nah," he said, shaking his head. *"I'd be wrong. Because you ain't even tried yet. Same with this job thing. How you gonna say you can't do something when you never even gave yourself a chance?"*

I didn't have an answer for that.

The First Step

The next day, I walked into the store and grabbed an application. My hands were still shaky. The doubt was still there.

But for the first time, I wondered if maybe—just maybe—those words I had always believed weren't the whole truth.

And if I didn't even know my father... maybe I didn't have to be like him at all.

End of Chapter Reflection

- **Malachi's childhood words come back to haunt him.** His mother's belief about his father makes him doubt his own ability to succeed.

- **Phillip offers a different perspective.** He challenges Malachi to think about where these beliefs come from and whether they're even real.

- **Malachi takes a small step forward.** He doesn't have all the confidence yet, but he starts questioning the words that held him back.

- **This sets up the next phase of his journey.** Malachi is slowly learning that he has a choice in what he believes about himself.

Chapter 9

Facing the Mirror

The job wasn't hard. Bagging groceries, stacking shelves, sweeping floors—I could do all of that with no problem. But every time I put on my name tag and stepped onto the floor, I felt like I was waiting for something to go wrong.

Like I didn't belong there.

Like I was proving something bad about myself just by trying.

I had been working for about two weeks when it finally happened.

I was at the register, bagging a customer's groceries, when I miscalculated how much weight the paper bags could hold. As soon as I lifted one off the counter, the bottom tore open, sending cans rolling across the floor.

I scrambled to pick them up, my face burning.

"Come on, man," my coworker muttered. *"Be careful."*

I muttered an apology, but my hands felt shaky. My mind raced.

"You're just like your father."

"He couldn't keep a job."

"You're always going to fail."

The words hit harder than the mistake itself.

I wanted to quit. Right there. Right then.

Phillip's Perspective

After work, I sat outside on the curb, staring at the pavement. I was so lost in my head, I didn't even hear Phillip walk up.

"Rough day?" he asked, taking a sip from his drink.

I let out a short laugh. *"You could say that."*

He sat down next to me. *"You gonna quit?"*

I frowned. *"What?"*

"You're thinking about it, aren't you?" he said, shrugging. *"Because of one bad moment?"*

I sighed. *"It's not just that. It's... everything. I just feel like I don't belong here. Like I'm proving everybody right."*

Phillip raised an eyebrow. *"Everybody? Or just the voices in your head?"*

I didn't answer.

"Look, man," he continued. *"You think the people who run this place never messed up before? You think your manager never dropped something, never rang up something wrong? Everybody makes mistakes. That's not what matters."*

"Then what does?" I asked.

"Whether or not you let one moment decide your future."

I let that sink in.

I had spent my whole life believing that one mistake meant failure. That one bad moment meant I wasn't good enough.

Maybe it was time to believe something different.

A Small Shift

The next day, I went back to work. The doubts were still there, but now… there was something else too.

A thought. A choice.

Maybe I didn't have to let one bad moment define me.

Maybe I wasn't just the words spoken over me.

Maybe I was something more.

End of Chapter Reflection

- Malachi's job experience brings back old insecurities. A small mistake makes him feel like a failure.
- Phillip helps him reframe failure. Instead of seeing one moment as proof of his worst fears, Malachi starts seeing it as just that—a moment.
- This sets up his turning point. Now he's realizing that *he* has the power to decide what defines him.

Chapter 10

The Choice to Believe

Rebecca could tell something was wrong before I even said a word.

We were sitting on the swings at the park, the same park we'd been coming to since sixth grade. The sun was setting, the air was cool, but inside my head, everything felt heavy.

"Alright, spill it," she said, kicking her feet slightly.

I sighed. *"It's nothing."*

"Malachi."

I shook my head. *"I don't know. It's just… I feel like I should be better by now."*

"Better how?"

"Better at work. Better at life. Better at believing in myself." I let out a small laugh, but it wasn't funny. *"I mean, I'm still overthinking everything. I mess up once, and I start thinking I'm proving everybody right. That I am a failure. That I am just like my dad."*

Rebecca frowned. *"You're not, though."*

"How do you know?"

She turned to face me. *"Because you're here, Malachi. You're trying. And if you were really all those things you think you are, you would've quit a long time ago."*

I looked down at my hands. *"I just wish I didn't still hear their voices in my head."*

"You're always going to hear them," she said softly. *"But you don't have to listen."*

I swallowed hard. *"I don't know how to stop."*

"Then stop letting their words be louder than your own."

I frowned, looking up at her.

"You've spent your whole life believing what other people said about you," she continued. *"But when are you going to believe you?"*

I didn't know what to say.

"You don't have to be the person they said you were," she said. *"You get to choose."*

A Shift in Perspective

For years, I had been fighting the words in my head, waiting for them to go away. But maybe that wasn't the answer.

Maybe the real battle wasn't about making the words disappear.

Maybe it was about choosing which ones to believe.

I looked at Rebecca, really looked at her, and realized something.

She had always believed in me.

She had always seen something in me that I couldn't see in myself.

And maybe, just maybe… it was time to start seeing it too.

"So what do I do?" I asked finally.

Rebecca smiled. *"You start small. When you hear those old words, don't fight them—replace them. Every time you think, 'I'm not good enough,' tell yourself, 'I am good enough.' Every time you hear, 'I can't,' tell yourself, 'I can.' And every time you think you don't deserve something good… remind yourself that you do."*

I nodded slowly, letting her words sink in.

It wasn't going to be easy.

But for the first time, I was ready to try.

End of Chapter Reflection

- Malachi finally acknowledges how much power he's given to negative words.
- Rebecca pushes him to take control over his own beliefs.
- A shift begins—he's no longer just fighting the words, but replacing them.
- This leads into the final chapter, where Malachi will start truly believing in himself and take a step forward in his relationship with Rebecca.

Chapter 11

A New Story Begins

For the first time in my life, I wasn't just hearing words—I was choosing them.

It wasn't perfect. The doubts still tried to creep in. The old voices still whispered in the back of my mind. But every time they did, I fought back.

"You're just like your father."

No, I'm not.

"You'll never be enough."

I already am.

"You don't deserve something good."

Yes, I do.

And the more I did it, the more I realized something.

I had been waiting for other people to tell me I was enough. Waiting for someone to prove it to me, to say the right thing at the right time, to fix the broken pieces inside me.

But the truth was, no one could do that for me.

I had to do it myself.

The Moment of Truth

It had been a few days since my conversation with Rebecca, and for the first time in a long time, I actually felt *okay*. Not perfect. Not completely fixed. But better.

So when I saw Rebecca sitting outside after school, scrolling through her phone, I made a decision.

"Hey," I said, walking up to her.

She glanced up and smiled. *"Hey, what's up?"*

I took a deep breath. *"You busy?"*

"Just waiting for my ride. Why?"

"Because I was thinking," I said, rubbing the back of my neck. *"We've been friends for a long time, right?"*

She gave me a suspicious look. *"Yeah... why do you sound nervous?"*

I chuckled. *"Because I am."*

"Malachi, just say it."

I exhaled. *"Okay. I was wondering if maybe, you know… you'd wanna go out with me sometime?"*

Rebecca blinked.

Then she smirked.

"Wow. Took you long enough."

I blinked back at her. *"Wait, what?"*

She rolled her eyes, laughing softly. *"Malachi… I've liked you. For years. I was just waiting for you to figure it out."*

Now *I* was the one who was speechless.

"You—what? Since when?"

She tilted her head, pretending to think. *"Let's see… remember in seventh grade when Jayla said you were cute?"*

I nodded slowly.

"Yeah, well, I may have encouraged her to tell you that because I wanted to see how you'd react."

My mouth dropped open. *"Wait—you set that up?"*

She laughed. *"Kinda."*

I shook my head. *"And what about when I got my first job? You acted like it was the biggest deal ever."*

"Because it was! But also… because I was proud of you. I knew you'd do it. I knew you could do it. I've always believed in you, Malachi. Always."

Her words hit me deeper than I expected.

For so long, I had convinced myself I wasn't good enough. That I wasn't worthy of something real. That nobody saw me the way I wanted to be seen.

But the truth was, someone had seen me. All along.

"So why didn't you say anything?" I asked, still trying to wrap my head around it.

Rebecca smiled softly. *"Because you weren't ready to believe it yet."*

I swallowed hard, nodding slowly.

She was right.

Maybe I hadn't been ready then.

But I was now.

"So…" I said, clearing my throat. *"Is that a yes?"*

Her eyes sparkled. *"Yeah, Malachi. That's a yes."*

The Final Lesson

As we walked together, I thought about how far I had come.

The words that had once held me back weren't completely gone. But they weren't in control anymore.

And now, for the first time in my life, I wasn't afraid of the future.

Because it wasn't about what other people said about me.

It was about the words I chose to believe.

And I was finally writing my own story.

End of Story Reflection

- **Malachi has fully embraced his growth.** He's still a work in progress, but now he's in control of his own thoughts.
- **He and Rebecca come together, not as saviors for each other, but as partners.** They both come from different struggles, but they've helped each other grow.
- **The story ends on a hopeful note.** Malachi's journey isn't over, but he's no longer stuck in the past—he's looking ahead.

Final Thought

"Words shape us. They can lift us up or break us down. But in the end, the most powerful words are the ones we choose to believe."

Conclusion

The Power of Words

If you've ever been hurt by words, if you've ever carried them in your mind long after they were spoken, then you know just how powerful they are.

Words can shape us. They can build confidence, or they can destroy it. They can encourage someone to chase their dreams, or they can convince someone to give up before they even try.

Like Malachi, many of us have believed words that weren't true. Words spoken in anger, in frustration, or by people who didn't understand the weight of what they were saying. But just like Malachi learned, we all have a choice.

We don't have to let the wrong words define us.

We can choose the words that lift us up.

We can replace the doubts with truths.

And most importantly, we can be mindful of the words *we* speak to others. Because just as words can tear someone down, they can also be the thing that saves them.

So I challenge you: **be intentional with your words.** Speak life into the people around you. Tell someone they matter. Tell them they are capable. Tell them something good about themselves—because you never know how much they might need to hear it.

A kind word spoken at the right time can change a person's whole story.

And maybe, just maybe… your words could be the reason someone starts believing in themselves again.

About Our Company

At **Build Our Kingdom Publishing** we bring stories like Malachi's to life to shine a light on real-life struggles that people face every day. Our mission is to create stories that **heal, inspire, and remind people that they are not alone.**

If this story resonated with you, we encourage you to share it, start a conversation, and most of all—**spread kindness intentionally.**

Because words don't just fade.

They stay.

And the right words, spoken at the right time, can change everything.

Allen Brown is the founder of **Allen Brown Ministries**, where his focus is on ministry outreach and publishing impactful spiritual and educational resources. His journey with Christ began in 1998 during a transformative Easter morning service, where he committed his life to the Lord and found salvation.

Married for over **26 years** to his devoted wife, **Melissa Brown**, Allen has raised four children while balancing his roles as a **minister, entrepreneur, and author**. His entrepreneurial journey began at the age of 12, and over the years, he has achieved significant business success, developing a passion for **leadership and financial stewardship**.

Through his publishing company, **Build Our Kingdom Publishing**, Allen shares insights on **spiritual growth, financial wisdom, and personal transformation**. His books aim to **empower readers to overcome life's challenges** while applying **godly principles** to achieve success in every aspect of life.

Your Words Hurt Me was born out of a deep understanding of how words shape us. Too often, people carry the weight of words spoken over them, believing them to be truths. This book serves as a reminder that **we don't have to be defined by the words of our past—we have the power to rewrite our own story.**

Allen attributes every achievement in his life to **God's faithfulness**, especially during times of struggle. His ministry emphasizes **trusting God, walking in faith, and applying biblical principles** to experience the fullness of His promises.

Beyond his ministry and writing, Allen treasures spending time with **Melissa and their four sons.** His life reflects a dedication to **faith, family, and service**, embodying his commitment to **helping others grow spiritually and live lives rooted in godly wisdom and purpose.**